Ideas and Books

Charlotte Mason

Foreword & Compilation © 2015 Deborah Taylor-Hough

ISBN: 1508964696
ISBN-13: 978-1508964698

DEDICATION

To parents and teachers everywhere who help develop a lifetime love of learning, an appreciation of great ideas, and the habit of reading in children.

CONTENTS

FOREWORD

One of the most valuable activities in our home while the children were growing up was reading often and at length from good books, "living" books, chosen carefully for their literary value—interesting, educational and pleasurable to read. Reading together was a cornerstone of our family time and homeschooling adventures. I began reading aloud to my children when they were just days old. I know they couldn't understand what I was reading yet, but I knew that the love and care communicated to them by being held in my arms as I read softly to them was a gift beyond measure. My oldest child's first word was BOOK. By the time my children were preschool age, they were all able to sit and listen to chapter books such as *Charlotte's Web*, *Little House on the Prairie*, or A.A. Milne's classic *Winnie-the-Pooh* series.

Charlotte Mason believed ideas were the primary means of true education, and the best way to discover ideas was by getting in touch directly with great thinkers by means of the books they'd written. Mason wanted children to develop the habit of reading—by being read to from great books from a young age—even before they learned the mechanics of reading and writing. She stated, "They begin their 'schooling' in 'letters' at six, and begin at the same time to learn mechanical reading and writing. A child does not lose by spending a couple of years in acquiring these because he is meanwhile 'reading' the Bible, history, geography, tales, with close attention and a remarkable power of reproduction, or rather, of translation into his own language; he is acquiring a copious vocabulary and the habit of consecutive speech. In a word, he is an educated child from the first, and his power of dealing with books, with several books in the course of a morning's 'school,' increases with his age."

I think all the reading together in our home did wonders for our family. It served as a treasured family activity, a foundation for a love of literature, an introduction to great minds and lofty ideas, a means for developing a strong command of the language, and an avenue for increased listening skills.

Deborah Taylor-Hough
Seattle, 2015

CHARLOTTE MASON

AN EDUCATIONAL MANIFESTO

"Studies serve for Delight, for Ornament, and for Ability."

Every child has a right of entry to several fields of knowledge.

Every normal child has an appetite for such knowledge.

This appetite or desire for knowledge is a sufficient stimulus for all school work, if the knowledge be fitly given.

There are four means of destroying the desire for knowledge:—

a) Too many oral lessons, which offer knowledge in a diluted form, and do not leave the child free to deal with it.

b) Lectures, for which the teacher collects, arranges, and illustrates matter from various sources; these often offer knowledge in too condensed and ready prepared a form.

c) Text-books compressed and recompressed from the big book of the big man.

d) The use of emulation and ambition as incentives to learning in place of the adequate desire for, and delight in, knowledge.

Children can be most fitly educated on *Things* and *Books*.

Things, *e.g.*—

- Natural obstacles for physical contention, climbing, swimming, walking, etc.
- Material to work in—wood, leather, clay, etc.
- Natural objects *in situ*—birds, plants, streams, stones, etc,
- Objects of art.
- Scientific apparatus, etc.

The value of this education by *Things* is receiving wide recognition, but intellectual education to be derived from *Books* is still for the most part to seek.

Every scholar of six years old and upwards should study with 'delight' *his own, living,* books on every subject in a pretty wide curriculum. Children between six and eight must for the most part have their books read to them.

This plan has been tried with happy results for the last twelve years in many home schoolrooms, and some other schools.

By means of the free use of books the mechanical difficulties of education—reading, spelling, composition, etc.—disappear, and studies prove themselves to be 'for delight, for ornament, and for ability.'

There is reason to believe that these principles are workable in all schools, Elementary and Secondary; that they tend in the working to simplification, economy, and discipline.

CHARLOTTE M. MASON

1

PARENTS AS INSPIRERS

The Life of the Mind Grows Upon Ideas

'Sow an act, reap a habit; sow a habit, reap a character;
sow a character, reap a destiny.'

It rests with the parents of the child to settle for the future man his ways of thinking, behaving, feeling, acting; his disposition, his particular talent; the manner of things upon which his thoughts shall run. Who shall fix limitations to the power of parents? The destiny of the child is ruled by his parents, because they have the virgin soil all to themselves. The first sowing must be at their hands, or at the hands of such as they choose to depute.

What do parents sow? *Ideas.* We cannot too soon recognize what is the sole educational seed in our hands, or how this seed is to be distributed. Parents are very jealous over the individuality of their children; they mistrust the tendency to develop all on the same plan; and this instinctive jealousy is right; supposing that education really did consist in systematised efforts to draw out every power that is in us, why, we should all develop on the same lines, be as like as 'two peas,' and (should we not?) die of weariness of one another. Some of us have an uneasy sense that things are tending towards this deadly sameness; but, indeed, the fear is groundless.

We may believe that the personality, the individuality of each of us, is too dear to God, and too necessary to a complete humanity, to be left at the mercy of empirics. We are absolutely safe, and the tenderest child is fortified against a battering-ram of educational forces.

'Education' an Inadequate Word

The problem of education is more complex than it seems at first sight, and well for us and the world that it is so. 'Education is a life'; you may stunt and starve and kill, or you may cherish and sustain; but the beating of the heart, the movement of the lungs, and the development of the faculties (are there any 'faculties'?) are only indirectly our care. The poverty of our thought on the subject of education is shown by the fact that we have no word which at all implies the sustaining of a *life*: education (*e*, out, and *ducere*, to lead, to draw) is very inadequate; it covers no more than those occasional gymnastics of the mind which correspond with those by which the limbs are trained: training (*trahere*) is almost synonymous, and upon these two words rests the misconception that the development and the exercise of the 'faculties' is the object of education (we must needs use the word for want of a better).

'Bringing-up'?

Our homely Saxon 'bringing-up' is nearer the truth, perhaps because of its very vagueness; any way, 'up' implies an *aim*, and 'bringing' an *effort*.

The happy phrase of Mr. Matthew Arnold—'Education is an atmosphere, a discipline, a life'—is perhaps the most complete and adequate definition of education we possess. It is a great thing to have said it; and our wiser posterity may see in that 'profound and exquisite remark' the fruition of a lifetime of critical effort.

An Adequate Definition

Observe how it covers the question from the three conceivable points of view. Subjectively, in the child, education is a life; objectively, as affecting the child, education is a discipline; relatively, if we may introduce a third term, as regards the environment of the child, education is an atmosphere. We shall attempt no more than to clear the ground a little, with a view to the subject of this chapter, 'Parents as Inspirers'—not 'modelers,' but 'inspirers.'

Method, a Way to an End

It is only as we recognise our limitations that our work becomes effective: when we see definitely what we are to do, what we can do, and what we cannot do, we set to work with confidence and courage; we have an end in view, and we make our way intelligently towards that end, and a *way to an end is method*. It rests with parents not only to give their children birth into the life of intelligence and moral power, but to sustain the higher life which they have borne.

That life, which we call education, receives only one kind of sustenance; it grows upon *ideas*. You may go through years of so-called 'education' without getting a single vital idea; and that is why many a well-fed body carries about a feeble, starved intelligence; and no society for the prevention of cruelty to children cries shame on the parents.

Some years ago I heard of a girl of fifteen who had spent two years at a school without taking part in a single lesson, and this by the express desire of her mother, who wished all her time and all her pains to be given to 'fancy needlework.' This, no doubt, is a survival (not of the fittest), but it is possible to pass even the Universities Local Examinations with credit, without ever having experienced that vital stir which marks the inception of an idea; and, if we have succeeded in escaping this disturbing influence, why, we have 'finished our education' when we leave school; we shut up our books and our minds, and remain pigmies in the dark forest of our own dim world of thought and feeling.

What is an Idea?

A live thing of the mind, according to the older philosophers, from Plato to Bacon, from Bacon to Coleridge. We say of an idea that it strikes us, impresses us, seizes us, takes possession of us, rules us; and our common speech is, as usual, truer to fact than the conscious thought which it expresses. We do not in the least exaggerate in ascribing this sort of action and power to an idea. We form an *ideal*—a, so to speak, embodied idea—and our ideal exercises the very strongest formative influence upon us. Why do you devote yourself to this pursuit, that cause? 'Because twenty years ago such and such an idea *struck* me,' is the sort of history which might be given of every purposeful life—every life devoted to the working out of an idea. Now is it not marvelous that, recognising as we do the potency of ideas, both the word and the conception it covers enter so little into our thought of education? Coleridge brings the conception of an 'idea' within the sphere of the scientific thought of today; not as that thought is expressed in *Psychology*—a term which he himself launched upon the world with an apology for it as an *insolens verbum*[2], but in that science of the correlation and interaction of mind and brain, which is at present rather clumsily expressed in such terms as 'mental physiology' and 'psycho-physiology.'

In his *Method* Coleridge gives us the following illustration of the rise and progress of an idea:—

Rise and Progress of an Idea

"We can recall no incident of human history that impresses the imagination more deeply than the moment when Columbus, on an unknown ocean, first perceived that startling fact, the change of the magnetic needle. How many such instances occur in history when the ideas of Nature (presented to chosen minds by a Higher Power than Nature herself) suddenly unfold, it were, in prophetic succession, systematic views destined to produce the most important revolutions in the state of man! The clear spirit of Columbus was doubtless eminently *methodical*. He saw distinctly that great leading idea which authorised the poor pilot to become a 'promiser of kingdoms.'

Genesis of an Idea

"Notice the genesis of such ideas—'presented to chosen minds by a Higher Power than Nature'; notice how accurately this history of an idea fits in with what we know of the history of great inventions and discoveries, with that of the ideas which rule our own lives; and how well does it correspond with that key to the origin of 'practical' ideas which we find elsewhere:—

"Doth the plowman plow continually to . . . open and break the clods of his ground? When he hath made plain the face thereof, doth he not cast abroad the fitches, and scatter the cumin, and put in the wheat in rows, and the barley in the appointed place, and the spelt in the border thereof? For his God doth instruct him aright, and doth teach him . . .

"Bread corn is ground; for he will not ever be threshing it . . . This also cometh forth from the Lord of hosts, which is wonderful in counsel and excellent in wisdom."

An Idea May Exist as an 'Appetency'

Ideas may invest as an atmosphere, rather than strike as a weapon. The idea may exist in a clear, distinct, definite form, as that of a circle in the mind of a geometrician; or it may be a mere instinct, a vague appetency towards something, . . . like the impulse which fills the young poet's eyes with tears, he knows not why: To excite this 'appetency towards something'—towards things lovely, honest, and or good report, is the earliest and most important ministry of the educator. How shall these indefinite ideas which manifest themselves in appetency be imparted? They are not to be given of set purpose, nor taken at set times. They are held in that thought-environment which surrounds the child as an atmosphere, which he breathes as his breath of life; and this atmosphere in which the child inspires his unconscious ideas of right living emanates from his parents. Every look of gentleness and tone of reverence, every word of kindness and act of help, passes into the thought-environment, the very atmosphere which the child breathes; he does not think of these things, may never think of them, but all his life long they excite that 'vague appetency towards something' out of which most of his actions spring. Oh, wonderful and dreadful presence of the little child in the midst!

A Child Draws Inspiration from the Casual Life Around Him

That he should take direction and inspiration from all the casual life about him, should make our poor words and ways the starting-point from which, and in the direction of which, he develops—this is a thought which makes the best of us hold our breath. There is no way of escape for parents; they must needs be as 'inspirers' to their children, because about them hangs, as its atmosphere about a planet the thought-environment of the child, from which he derives those enduring ideas which express themselves as a life-long 'appetency' towards things sordid or things lovely, things earthly or divine.

Order and Progress of Definite Ideas

Let us now hear Coleridge on the subject of those definite ideas which are not inhaled as air; but conveyed as meat to the mind:—

- "From the first, or initiative idea, as from a seed, successive ideas germinate."

- "Events and images, the lively and spirit-stirring machinery of the external world, are like light and air and moisture to the seed of the mind, which would else rot and perish"

- "The paths in which we may pursue a methodical course are manifold, and at the head of each stands its peculiar and guiding idea."

- "Those ideas are as regularly subordinate in dignity as the paths to which they point are various and eccentric in direction. The world has suffered much, in modern times, from a subversion of the natural and necessary order of Science . . . from summoning reason and faith to the bar of that limited physical experience to which, by the true laws or method, they owe no obedience."

- "Progress follows the path of the idea from which it sets out; requiring, however, a constant wakefulness of mind to keep it within the due limits of its course. Hence the orbits of thought, so to speak, must differ among themselves as the initiative ideas differ."

Platonic Doctrine of Ideas

Have we not here the corollary to, and the explanation of that law of unconscious cerebration which results in our 'ways of thinking,' which shapes our character, rules our destiny? Thoughtful minds consider that the new light which biology is throwing upon the laws of mind is bringing to the front once more the Platonic doctrine, that "An idea is a distinguishable power, self-affirmed, and seen in its unity with the Eternal Essence."

Ideas Alone Matter in Education

The whole subject is profound, but as practical as it is profound. We must disabuse our minds of the theory that the functions of education are, in the main, gymnastic. In the early years of the child's life it makes, perhaps, little apparent difference whether his parents start with the notion that to educate is to fill a receptacle, inscribe a tablet, mould plastic matter, or nourish a life; but in the end we shall find that only those *ideas* which have fed his life are taken into the being of the child; all the rest is thrown away, or worse, is like sawdust in the system, an impediment and an injury to the vital processes.

How the Educational Formula Should Run

This is, perhaps, how the educational formula should run:

1. Education is a life; that life is sustained on ideas; ideas are of spiritual origin; and, *'God has made us so'* that we get them chiefly as we convey them to one another.

2. The duty of parents is to sustain a child's inner life with ideas as they sustain his body with food. The child is an eclectic; he may choose this or that; therefore, in the morning sow thy seed, and in the evening withhold not thy hand, for thou knowest not which shall prosper, whether this or that, or whether they both shall be alike good.

3. The child has affinities with evil as well as with good; therefore, hedge him about from any chance lodgment of evil ideas.

4. The initial idea begets subsequent ideas; therefore, take care that children get right primary ideas on the great relations and duties of life.

5. Every study, every line of thought, has its 'guiding idea'; therefore, the study of a child makes for living education in proportion as it is quickened by the guiding idea 'which stands at the head.'

2

THE ROLE OF THE EDUCATOR

The Educator Should Form Habits

'One custom overcometh another,' said Thomas a' Kempis, and that is all we have to say; only, physiologists have made clear to us the *rationale* of this law of habit. We know that to form in his child right habits of thinking and behaving is a parent's chief duty, and that this can be done for every child definitely and within given limits of time.

The Educator Should Nourish with Ideas

To nourish a child daily with loving, right, and noble ideas we believe to be the parent's next duty. The child having once received the Idea will assimilate it in his own way, and work it into the fabric of his life; and a single sentence from his mother's lips may give him a bent that will make him, or may tend to make him, painter or poet, statesman or philanthropist. The object of lessons should be in the main twofold: to train a child in certain mental habits, as attention, accuracy, promptness, etc., and to nourish him with ideas which may bear fruit in his life.

Our Main Objects

There are other educational principles which we bear in mind and work out, but for the moment it is worthwhile for us to concentrate our thought upon the fact that one of our objects is to accentuate the importance of education under the two heads of the *formation of habits* and the *presentation of ideas*; and, as a corollary, to recognise that the *development* of *faculties* is not a supreme object with the cultivated classes, because this is work which has been done for their children in a former generation.

We Recognise Material and Spiritual Principles of Human Nature

But how does all this work? Is it practical? Is it the question of to-day? It must needs be practical because it gives the fullest recognition to the two principles of human nature, the *material* and the *spiritual*. We are ready to concede all that the most advanced biologist would ask of us. Does he say, 'Thought is only a mode of motion?'

If so, we are not dismayed. We know that ninety-nine out of a hundred thoughts that pass through our minds are involuntary, the inevitable result of those modifications of the brain tissue which habit has set up. The mean man thinks mean thoughts, the magnanimous man great thoughts, because we all think as we are accustomed to think, and Physiology shows us why. On the other hand, we recognise that greater is the spirit within us than the matter which it governs. Every habit has its beginning. The beginning is the *idea* which comes with a stir and takes possession of us.

We Recognise the Supreme Educator

The idea is the motive power of life, and it is because we recognise the spiritual potency of the idea that we are able to bow reverently before the fact that God the Holy Spirit is Himself the Supreme Educator, dealing with each of us severally in the things we call sacred and those we call secular. We lay ourselves open to the spiritual impact of ideas, whether these be conveyed by the printed page, the human voice, or whether they reach us without visible sign.

Studies are Valued as They Present Fruitful Ideas

But ideas may be evil or may be good; and to choose between the ideas that present themselves is, as we have been taught, the one responsible work of a human being. It is the power of choice that we would give our children. We ask ourselves, 'Is there any fruitful idea underlying this or that study that the children are engaged in?' We divest ourselves of the notion that to develop the faculties is the chief thing; and a 'subject' which does not rise out of some great thought of life we usually reject as not nourishing, not fruitful; while we usually, but not invariably, retain those studies which give exercise in habits of clear and orderly thinking. We have some gymnastics of the mind whose object is to exercise what we call faculties as well as to train in the habit of clear and ordered thinking. Mathematics, grammar, logic, etc., are not purely disciplinary; they do develop, if a bull may be allowed intellectual muscle. We by no means reject the familiar staples of education, in the school sense, but we prize them even more for the record of intellectual habits they leave in the brain tissue than for their distinct value in developing certain 'faculties.'

Nature-Knowledge

Thus our first thought with regard to Nature-knowledge is that the child should have a living personal acquaintance with the things he sees. It concerns us more that he should know bistort from persicaria, hawkweed from dandelion, and where to find this and that, and how it looks, living and growing, than that he should talk about *epigynous* and *hypogynous*. All this is well in its place, but should come quite late, after the child has seen and studied the living growing thing *in situ*, and has copied colour and gesture as best he can.

Object-Lessons

So of object-lessons; we are not anxious to develop his observing powers on little bits of everything, which he shall describe as opaque, brittle, malleable, and so on. We would prefer not to take the edge off his curiosity in this way; we should rather leave him receptive and respectful for one of those opportunities for asking questions and engaging in talk with his parents about the lock in the river, the mowing machine, the ploughed field, which offer real seed to the mind of a child, and do not make him a priggish little person able to tell all about it.

We Trust Much to Good Books

Once more, we know that there is a storehouse of thought wherein we may find all the great ideas that have moved the world. We are above all things anxious to give the child the key to this storehouse. The education of the day, it is said, does not produce *reading* people. We are determined that the children shall love books, therefore we do not interpose ourselves between the book and the child. We read him his *Tanglewood Tales*, and when he is a little older his *Plutarch*, not trying to break up or water down, but leaving the child's mind to deal with the matter as it can.

We Do Not Recognise 'Child-Nature'

We endeavour that all our teaching and treatment of children shall be on the lines of nature, their nature and ours, for we do not recognise what is called 'Child-nature.' We believe that children are human beings at their best and sweetest, but also at their weakest and least wise. We are careful not to dilute life for them, but to present such portions to them in such quantities as they can readily receive.

We are Tenacious of Individuality:
We Consider Proportion

In a word, we are very tenacious of the dignity and individuality of our children. We recognise steady, regular growth with no *transition* stage. This teaching is up to date, but it is as old as common sense. Our claim is that our common sense rests on a basis of Physiology, that we show a reason for all that we do, and that we recognise 'the science of the proportion of things,' put the first thing foremost, do not take too much upon ourselves, but leave time and scope for the workings of Nature and of a higher Power than Nature herself.

We Think Children Have a Right
to Knowledge

Much guidance and stimulation are afforded by another principle. We are not anxious to contend with Kant that the mind possesses certain *a priori* knowledge; nor with Hume that it holds innate ideas. The more satisfying proposition seems to be that the mind has, as it were, prehensile adaptations to each department of universal knowledge. We find that children lay hold of all knowledge which is fitly presented to them with avidity, and therefore we maintain that a wide and generous curriculum is due to them.

3

THE MATTER AND METHOD OF LESSONS

Home: The Best Growing-Ground for Young Children

Whatever be the advantages of *Kindergarten* or other schools for little children, the home schoolroom ought to be the best growing-ground for them. And doubtless it would be so, were the mother at liberty to devote herself to the instruction of her children; but this she is seldom free to do. If she can live in a town, she can send them to school when they are six; if in the country, she must have a governess; and the difficulty is to get a woman who is not only acquainted with the subjects she undertakes to teach, but who understands in some measure the nature of the child and the art and objects of education; a woman capable of making the very most of the children without waste of power or of time.

Such a *rara avis* [rare bird] does not present herself in answer to every advertisement; and in default of a trained teacher, the mother must undertake to *train* the governess—that is, she may supplement with her own insight the scanty knowledge and experience of the young teacher. 'I wish the children to be taught to read, thus and thus, because _____': or, 'to learn history in such a way that the lessons may have such and such effects.' Half an hour's talk of this kind with a sensible governess will secure a whole month's work for the children, so well directed that much is done in little time, and the widest possible margin secured for play and open-air exercise.

Three Questions for the Mother

But if the mother is to inoculate the governess with her views as to the teaching of writing, French, geography, she must, herself, have definite views. She must ask herself seriously, *Why* must the children learn at all? *What* should they learn? And, *How* should they learn it? If she take the trouble to find a definite and thoughtful answer to each of these three queries, she will be in a position to direct her children's studies; and will, at the same time, be surprised to find that three-fourths of the time and labour ordinarily spent by the child at his lessons is lost time and wasted energy.

Children Learn to Grow

Why must the child learn? Why do we eat? Is it not in order that the body may live and grow and be able to fulfil its functions? Precisely so must the mind be sustained and developed by means of the food convenient for it, the mental *pabulum* of assimilated knowledge. Again, the body is developed not only by means of proper sustenance, but by the appropriate exercise of each of its members. A young mother remarked to me the other day, that before her marriage she had such slender arms she never liked to exhibit them; but a strong five-months-old baby had cured her of that; she could toss and lift him with ease, and could now show well-rounded arms with anybody: and just as the limbs grow strong with exercise, so does intellectual effort with a given power of the mind make that power effective.

People are apt to overlook the fact that *mind* must have its aliment—we learn that we may *know*, not that we may *grow*; hence the parrot-like saying of lessons, the cramming of ill-digested facts for examinations, all the ways of taking in knowledge which the mind does not assimilate.

Doctoring of the Material of Knowledge

Specialists, on the other hand, are apt to attach too much importance to the several exercise of the mental 'faculties.' We come across books on teaching, with lessons elaborately drawn up, in which certain work is assigned to the perspective faculties, certain work to the imagination, to the judgment, and so on. Now this doctrine of the faculties, which rests on a false analogy between the mind and the body, is on its way to the limbo where the phrenologist's 'bumps' now rest in peace.

The mind would appear to be one and indivisible, and endowed with manifold powers; and this sort of doctoring of the material of knowledge is unnecessary for the healthy child, whose mind is capable of self-direction, and of applying itself to its proper work upon the parcel of knowledge delivered to it. Almost any subject which common sense points out as suitable for the instruction of children will afford exercise for all their powers, if properly presented.

Children Learn to Get Ideas

The child must learn, in the second place, in order that *ideas* may be freely sown in the fruitful soil of his mind. '*Idea*, the image or picture formed by the mind of anything external, whether sensible or spiritual.'—so, the dictionary; therefore, if the business of teaching be to furnish the child with ideas, any teaching which does not leave him possessed of a new mental image has, by so far, missed its mark.

Now, just think of the listless way in which the children too often drag through reading and tables, geography and sums, and you will see that it is a rare thing for any part of any lesson to flash upon them with the vividness which leaves a mental picture behind. It is not too much to say that a morning in which a child receives no new idea is a morning wasted, however closely the little student has been kept at his books.

Ideas Grow and Produce After Their Kind

For the dictionary appears to me to fall short of the truth in its definition of the term '*idea*.' An idea is more than an image or picture; it is, so to speak, a spiritual germ endowed with vital force—with power, that is, to grow, and to produce after its kind. It is the very nature of an idea to grow: as the vegetable germ secretes that which it lives by, so, fairly implant an idea in the child's mind, and it will secrete its own food, grow, and bear fruit in the form of a succession of kindred ideas.

We know from our own experience that, let our attention be forcibly drawn to some public character, some startling theory, and for days after we are continually hearing or reading matter which bears on this one subject, just as if all the world were thinking about what occupies our thoughts: the fact being, that the new idea we have received is in the act of growth, and is reaching out after its appropriate food. This process of *feeding* goes on with peculiar avidity in childhood, and the growth of an idea in the child is proportionably rapid.

Scott and Stephenson Worked with Ideas

Sir Walter Scott got an idea, a whole group of ideas, out of the Border tales and ballads, the folklore of the country-side, on which his boyhood was nourished: his ideas grew and brought forth, and the Waverley novels are the fruit they bore. George Stephenson made little clay engines with his playmate, Thomas Tholoway; by-and-by, when he was an engineman, he was always watching his engine, cleaning it, studying it; an engine was his dominant idea, and it developed into no less a thing than the locomotive.

Value of Dominant Ideas

But how does this theory of the vital and fruitful character of ideas bear upon the education of the child? In this way: give your child a single valuable *idea*, and you have done more for his education than if you had laid upon his mind the burden of bushels of information; for the child who grows up with a few dominant ideas has his self-education provided for, his career marked out.

Lessons Must Furnish Ideas

In order for the reception of an idea, the mind must be in an attitude of eager attention. One thing more: a single idea may be a possession so precious in itself, so fruitful, that the parent cannot fitly allow the child's selection of ideas to be a matter of chance; his *lessons* should furnish him with such ideas as shall make for his further education.

Children Learn to Get Knowledge

But it is not only to secure due intellectual growth and the furnishing his mind with ideas, that the child must learn: the common notion, that he learns for the sake of getting knowledge, is also a true one so much so, that no knowledge should be so precious as that gained in childhood, no later knowledge should be so clearly chronicled on the brain, nor so useful as the foundation of that to follow. At the same time, the child's capacity for knowledge is very limited; his mind is, in this respect at least, but a little phial with a narrow neck; and, therefore, it behooves the parent or teacher to pour in only of the best.

Diluted Knowledge

But, poor children, they are too often badly used by their best friends in the matter of the knowledge offered them. Grown-up people who are not mothers talk and think far more childishly than the child does in their efforts to approach his mind. If a child talks twaddle, it is because his elders are in the habit of talking twaddle to him; leave him to himself, and his remarks are wise and sensible so far as his small experience guides him.

Mothers seldom talk down to their children; they are too intimate with the little people, and have, therefore, too much respect for them: but professional teachers, whether the writers of books or the givers of lessons are too apt to present a single grain of pure knowledge in a whole gallon of talk, imposing upon the child the labour of discerning the grain and of extracting it from the worthless flood.

Dr. Arnold's Knowledge as a Child

On the whole, the children who grow up amongst their elders and are not provided with what are called children's books at all, fare the better on what they are able to glean for themselves from the literature of grown-up people. Thus it is told of Dr. Thomas Arnold that when he was three years old he received as a present from his father of Smollett's *History of England* as a reward for the accuracy with which he went through the stories connected with the portraits and pictures of the successive reigns—an amusement which probably laid the foundation of the great love for history which distinguished him in after life.

When occupying the professorial chair at Oxford, he made quotations, we are told, from Dr. Joseph Priestley's *Lectures on History*—verbally accurate quotations, we may believe, for such was the habit of his mind; besides, a child has little skill in recasting his matter—and that, though he had not had the book in his hands since he was a child of eight. No doubt he was an exceptional child; and all I maintain is, that had his reading been the sort of diluted twaddle which is commonly thrust upon children, it would have been *impossible* for him to cite passages a week, much less some two score years, after the reading.

Literature Proper for Children

This sort of weak literature for the children, both in any story and lesson books, is the result of a reactionary process. Not so long ago the current impression was that the children had little understanding, but prodigious memory for facts; dates, numbers, rules, catechisms of knowledge, much information in small parcels, was supposed to be the fitting material for a child's education. We have changed all that, and put into the children's hands lesson-books with pretty pictures and easy talk, almost as good as story-books; but we do not see that, after all, we are but giving the same little pills of knowledge in the form of a weak and copious diluent.

Teachers, and even parents, who are careful enough about their children's diet, are so reckless as to the sort of mental aliment offered to them, that I am exceedingly anxious to secure consideration for this question, of the lessons and literature proper for the little people.

Four Tests Which Should Be Applied to Children's Lessons

We see, then, that the children's lessons should provide material for their mental growth, should exercise the several powers of their minds, should furnish them with fruitful ideas, and should afford them knowledge, really valuable for its own sake, accurate, and interesting, of the kind that the child may recall as a man with profit and pleasure.

Before applying these tests to the various subjects in which children are commonly instructed, may I remind you of two or three points which I have endeavoured to establish elsewhere:—

Resume of Six Points—

(a) That the knowledge most valuable to the child is that which he gets with his own eyes and ears and fingers (under direction) in the open air.

(b) That the claims of the schoolroom should not be allowed to encroach on the child's right to long hours daily for exercise and investigation.

(c) That the child should be taken daily, if possible, to scenes—moor or meadow, park, common, or shore—where he may find new things to examine, and so add to his store of real knowledge. That the child's observation should be directed to flower or boulder, bird or tree; that, in fact, he should be employed in gathering the common information which is the basis of scientific knowledge.

(d) That play, vigorous healthful play, is, in its turn, fully as important as lessons, as regards both bodily health and brain-power.

(e) That the child, though under supervision, should be left much to himself—both that he may go to work in his own way on the ideas that he receives, and also that he may be the more open to natural influences.

(f) That the happiness of the child is the condition of his progress; that his lessons should be joyous, and that occasions of friction in the schoolroom are greatly to be deprecated.

4

AN ADEQUATE THEORY OF EDUCATION

A Human Being

I have laid before the reader, as a working hypothesis,—that man is homogeneous, a spiritual being invested with a body—capable of responding to spiritual impulses, the organ by which he expresses himself, the vehicle by which he receives impressions, and the medium by which he establishes relations with what we call the material world;—that will, conscience, affection, reason, are not the various parts of a composite whole, but are different modes of action of the person.

His Capacities—That he is capable of many relations and consequently of many modes of action; that, given the due relations, his power of expansion in these relations appears to be, not illimitable, but, so far as we know, as yet unlimited.

His Limitations—But that, deprived of any or all of the relations proper to him, a human being has no power of self-development in these directions; though he would appear not to lose any of his capacity for these relations.

His Education.—Again, that any relation once initiated leaves, so to speak, an organic memory of itself in the nervous tissue of the brain; that in this physical registration of an experience or a thought, or of the memory of an experience or a thought, lies the possibility of habit; that some nine-tenths of our life run upon lines of habit; and that, therefore, in order to educate, we must know something of both the psychological and physiological history of a habit, how to initiate it and how to develop it; and, finally, that a human being under education has two functions—the formation of habits and the assimilation of ideas.

The Behaviour of Ideas

Physiologists and 'rational psychologists' have made the basis of habit pretty plain to us. All who run may read. The nature, functions, and behaviour of ideas, and how ideas have power in their impact upon the cerebral hemisphere to make some sort of sensible impression—all this is matter as to which we are able only to make 'guesses at truth.' But this need not dismay us, for such other ultimate facts as sleep and life and death are equally unexplained. In every department of science we are brought up before facts which we have to assume as the bases of our so-called science. Where a working hypothesis is necessary, all we can do is to assume those bases that seem to us the most adequate and the most fruitful. Let us say with Plato that an idea is an entity, a live thing of the mind.

No One Can Beget an Idea by Himself

Apparently no one has power to beget an idea by himself; it appears to be the progeny of two minds. So-and-so 'put it in my head,' we say, and that is the history of all ideas—the most simple and the most profound. But, once begotten, the idea seems to survive indefinitely. It is painted in a picture, written in a book, carved into a chair, or only spoken to someone who speaks it again, who speaks it again, who speaks it again, so that it goes on being spoken, for how long? Who knows! Nothing so strikes the student of history as the persistent way in which ideas recur, except the way in which they elude observation until occasion calls them forth.

Our natural progeny may indeed die and be buried; but of this spiritual progeny of ideas, who may forecast the history or foretell the end?

Certain Persons Attract Certain Ideas

Perhaps we may be allowed this further hypothesis—that, as an idea comes of the contact of two minds, the idea of another is no more than a *notion* to us until it has undergone a process of generation within us; and for that reason different ideas appeal to different minds—not at all because the ideas themselves have an independent desire to club into 'apperception masses,' but because certain persons have in themselves, by inheritance, may we assume, that which is proper to attract certain ideas.

To illustrate invisible things by visible, let us suppose that the relation is something like that between the pollen and the ovule it is to fertilise. The ways of carrying the pollen are various, not to say promiscuous, but there is nothing haphazard in the result. The right pollen goes to the right ovule and the plant bears seed after its kind; even so, the person brings forth ideas after his kind.

The Idea that 'Strikes' Us

The *crux* of the situation is: how can an emanation so purely spiritual as an idea make an impression upon even the most delicate material substance? We do not know. We have some little demonstration that it is so in the fact of the score of reflex actions by which we visibly respond to an idea that 'strikes' us. The eye brightens, the pulse quickens, the colour rises, the whole person becomes vitalised, capable, strenuous, no longer weighed down by this clog of flesh. Every habit we have formed has had its initial idea, and every idea we receive is able to initiate a habit of thought and of action.

Every human being has the power of communicating notions to other human beings; and, after he is dead, this power survives him in the work he has done and the words he has said. How illimitable is life! That the divine Spirit has like intimate power of corresponding with the human spirit, needs not to be urged, once we recognise ourselves as spiritual beings at all.

Expansion and Activity of the Person

Nor does this teeming population of ideas arise to us without order and without purpose beyond the scope of our busy efforts and intentions. It would seem as if a new human being came into the world with unlimited capacity for manifold relations, with a tendency to certain relations in preference to certain others, but with no degree of adaptation to these relations. To secure that adaptation and the expansion and activity of the person, along the lines of the relations most proper to him, is the work of education; to be accomplished by the two factors of ideas and habits. Every relation must be initiated by its own 'captain' idea, sustained upon fitting ideas; and wrought into the material substance of the *person* by its proper habits. This is the field before us.

The Sustenance of Living Ideas

The intellectual life, like every manner of spiritual life, has but one food whereby it lives and grows—the sustenance of living ideas. It is not possible to repeat this too often or too emphatically, for perhaps we err more in this respect than any other in bringing up children. We feed them upon the white ashes out of which the last spark of the fire of original thought has long since died. We give them second-rate story books, with stale phrases, stale situations, shreds of other people's thoughts, stalest of stale sentiments. They complain that they know how the story will end! But that is not all; they know how every dreary page will unwind itself. I saw it stated the other day that children do not care for poetry, that a stirring narrative in verse is much more to their taste. They do like the tale, no doubt, but poetry appeals to them on other grounds, and Shelley's *Skylark* will hold a child entranced sooner than any moving anecdote. As for children's art, we hang the nursery with 'Christmas Number' pictures, and their books are illustrated on a lower level still. In regard to book illustrations, we are improving a little, but still there is room.

Children's Literature

The subject of 'Children's Literature' has been well threshed out, and only one thing remains to be said,—children have no natural appetite for twaddle, and a special literature for children is probably far less necessary than the book sellers would have us suppose. Out of any list of 'the hundred best books,' I believe that seventy-five would be well within the range of children of eight or nine. They would delight in *Rasselas*, *Eöthen* would fascinate them as much as *Robinson Crusoe*, the *Faëry Queen*, with its allegory and knightly adventures and sense of free moving in woodland scenery, would exactly fall in with their humour. What they want is to be brought into touch with living thought of the best, and their intellectual life feeds upon it with little meddling on our part.

Independent Intellectual Development of Children

We do not sufficiently recognise the independent intellectual development of children which it is our business to initiate and direct, but not to control or dominate. I know a little girl of nine who pined every day because the poems of Tennyson which she loved best were not to be found in the volumes of the larger works, which were all the house she was visiting at afforded. She literally missed her favourite poems as a child would miss a meal; and why not? The intellectual appetite is just as actual and just as exigeant as bodily hunger; more so, alas, in some cases.

Miss Martineau has a charming story of the intellectual awakening of "a schoolboy of *ten* who laid himself down, back uppermost, with Southey's *Thalaba* before him, on the first day of the Easter holidays, and turned over the leaves, notwithstanding his inconvenient position, as fast as if he were looking for something, till in a few hours it was done, and he was off with it to the public library, bringing back the *Curse of Keharna*. Thus he went on with all Southey's poems and some others through his short holidays, scarcely moving voluntarily all those days except to run to the library. He came out of the process so changed that none of his family could help being struck by it. The expression of his eye, the cast of his countenance, his use of words, and his very gait were changed. In ten days he had advanced years in intelligence; and I have always thought that this was the turning-point of his life. His parents wisely and kindly let him alone, aware that school would presently put an end to all excess in the new indulgence."

As there is no religious conversion for the child who has always been brought up in the conscious presence of God, so parents who have always satisfied the intellectual craving of their children must needs forego the delight of watching a literary awakening. A little girl brought up on temperance principles, who said, 'I am so sorry my father isn't a drunkard,' that she might rejoice in his reformation, put the case for us very plainly.

Self-Selection and Self-Appropriation

Given a bountiful repast of ideas, the process of natural selection soon begins. Tennyson with his—

> "Our elm tree's ruddy-hearted blossom-flake is fluttering
>   down,"
> "Ruby-budded lime,"
> "Black as ash-buds in the front of March,"

has done more to make field botanists than ever the Science and Art Department was able to undo with its whole apparatus of lectures and examinations.

Here, again, Browning gives us a poet's impulse to a nature student:—

> "By boulder stones where lichens mock
> The marks on a moth, and small ferns fit
> Their teeth to the polished block."

Ideas of nature, of life, love, duty, heroism,—these children find and choose for themselves from the authors they read, who do more for their education than any deliberate teaching; just for this reason, that these vital ideas are self-selected and self-appropriated.

I shall touch later upon the burning question of a curriculum which shall furnish children, not with dry bones of fact, but with fact clothed upon with the living flesh, breathed into by the vital spirit of quickening ideas. A teacher objected the other day that it was difficult to teach from Freeman's *Old English History*, because there were so many stories; not perceiving that the stories were the living history, while all the rest was dead.

Inherited Parsimony in Lesson-books

I should like to say here that a sort of unconscious, inherited parsimony, coming down to us from the days when incomes were smaller and books were fewer, sometimes causes parents to restrict their children unduly in the matter of lesson-books—living books, varied from time to time, and not thumbed over from one schoolroom generation to another until the very sight of them is a weariness to the flesh. But the subject of the intellectual sustenance of children upon ideas is so large and important that I must content myself with bald suggestions.

Further considered, such subjects as the following might be useful:

- Children's tastes in Fiction, in Poetry, in books of Travel and Adventure, in History, in Biography (most stimulating subject).
- Ideas of life and conduct that children assimilate from their reading.
- Ideas of duty assimilated in the same way.
- Ideas of nature that children seize.
- The leading, vitalising ideas in subjects of school study, as geography, grammar, history, astronomy, Ceasar's Commentaries, etc., etc.

Let me conclude with a wise sentence of Coleridge's concerning the method of Plato, which should be always present to the minds of persons engaged in the training of children:—

Plato's Educational Aim:

"He desired not to assist in storing the passive mind with the various sorts of knowledge most in request, as if the human soul were a mere repository or banqueting room, but to place it in such relations of circumstance as should gradually excite its vegetating and germinating powers to produce new fruits of thought, new conceptions and imaginations and ideas."

5

EDUCATION, THE SCIENCE OF RELATIONS

We are Educated by Our Intimacies

"But who shall parcel out
His intellect by geometric rules,
Split like a province into round and square?
Who knows the individual hour in which
His habits were first sown, even as a seed?
Who that shall point as with a wand and say
'This portion of the river of my mind
Came from yon fountain'? "—*Prelude.*

I need not again insist upon the nature of our educational tools. We know well that "Education is an atmosphere, a discipline, a life." In other words, we know that parents and teachers should know how to make sensible use of a child's *circumstances* (atmosphere) to forward his sound education; should train him in the discipline of the *habits* of the good life; and should nourish his life with *ideas*, the food upon which personality waxes strong.

Only Three Educational Instruments

These three we believe to be the only instruments of which we may make lawful use in the upbringing of children; and any short cut we take by trading on their sensibilities, emotions, desires, passions, will bring us and our children to grief. The reason is plain; habits, ideas, and circumstances are external, and we may all help each other to get the best that is to be had of these; but we may not meddle directly with the personality of child or man. We may not work upon his vanity, his fears, his love, his emulation, or anything that is his by very right, anything that goes to make him a person.

Our Limitations

Most thinking people are in earnest about the bringing up of children; but we are in danger of taking too much upon us, and of not recognising the limitations which confine us to the outworks of personality. Children and grown-up persons are the same, with a difference; and a thoughtful writer has done us good service by carefully tracing the method of our Lord's education of the Twelve. "Our Lord," says this author, "reverenced whatever the learner had in him of his own, and was tender in fostering this native growth— … Men, in His eyes, were not mere clay in the hands of the potter, matter to be moulded to shape. They were organic beings, each growing from within, with a life of his own—a personal life which was exceedingly precious in His and His Father's eyes—and He would foster this growth so that it might take after the highest type."

We Temper Life too Much for Children

I am not sure that we let life and its circumstances have free play about children. We temper the wind too much to the lambs; pain and sin, want and suffering, disease and death—we shield them from the knowledge of these at all hazards. I do not say that we should wantonly expose the tender souls to distress, but that we should recognise that life has a ministry for them also; and that Nature provides them with a subtle screen, like that of its odour to a violet, from damaging shocks. Some of us will not even let children read fairy tales because these bring the ugly facts of life too suddenly before them. It is worthwhile to consider Wordsworth's experience on this point. Indeed I do not think we make enough use of two such priceless boons to parents and teachers as the educational autobiographies we possess of the two great philosophers, Wordsworth and Ruskin.

Fairy Lore a Screen and Shelter

The former tells us how, no sooner had he gone to school at Hawkshead, than the body of a suicide was recovered from Esthwaite Lake; a ghastly tale, but full of comfort as showing how children are protected from shock. The little boy was there and saw it all; —

> "Yet no soul-debasing fear,
> Young as I was, a child not nine years old,
> Possessed me, for my inner eye had seen
> Such sights before, among the shining streams
> Of fairyland, the forests of romance:
> Their spirit hallowed the sad spectacle
> With decoration of ideal grace;
> A dignity, a smoothness, like the works
> Of Grecian art, and purest poesy."

It is delightful to know, on the evidence of a child who went through it, that a terrible scene was separated from him by an atmosphere of poetry—a curtain woven of fairy lore by his etherealising imagination.

But we may run no needless risks, and must keep a quiet, matter-of-fact tone in speaking of fire, shipwreck, or any terror. There are children to whom the thought of Joseph in the pit is a nightmare; and many of us elders are unable to endure a ghastly tale in newspaper or novel. All I would urge is a natural treatment of children, and that they be allowed their fair share of life, such as it is; prudence and not panic should rule our conduct towards them.

Spontaneous Living

The laws of habit are, we know, laws of God, and the forming of good and the hindering of evil habits are among the primary duties of a parent. But it is just as well to be reminded that habits, whether helpful or hindering, only come into play occasionally, while a great deal of spontaneous living is always going on towards which we can do no more than drop in vital ideas as opportunity occurs. All this is old matter, and I must beg the reader to forgive me for reminding him again that our educational instruments remain the same. We may not leave off the attempt to form good habits with tact and care, to suggest fruitful ideas, without too much insistence, and to make wise use of circumstances.

On What Does Fullness of Living Depend?

What is education after all? An answer lies in the phrase— *Education is the Science of Relations.* I do not use this phrase, let me say once more, in the Herbartian sense—that things are related to each other, and we must be careful to pack the right things in together, so that, having got into the brain of a boy, each thing may fasten on its cousins, and together they may make a strong clique or 'apperception mass.' What we are concerned with is the fact that we personally have relations with all that there is in the present, all that there has been in the past, and all that there will be in the future—with all above us and all about us—and that fullness of living, expansion, expression, and serviceableness, for each of us, depend upon how far we apprehend these relationships and how many of them we lay hold of.

George Herbert Says Something of What I Mean

"Man is all symmetry,
Full of proportions, one limb to another,
And *all to all the world besides*;
Each part may call the farthest brother,
For head with foot hath private amity,
And *both with moons and tides.*

Every child is heir to an enormous patrimony, heir to all the ages, inheritor of all the present. The question is, what are the formalities (educational, not legal) necessary to put him in possession of that which is his? You perceive the point of view is shifted, and is no longer subjective, but objective, as regards the child.

The Child a Person

We do not talk about developing his faculties, training his moral nature, guiding his religious feelings, educating him with a view to his social standing or his future calling. The joys of 'child-study' are not for us. We take the child for granted, or rather, we take him as we find him—a person with an enormous number of healthy affinities, embryo attachments; and we think it is our chief business to give him a chance to make the largest possible number of these attachments valid.

An Infant's Self-Education

An infant comes into the world with a thousand such embryonic feelers, which he sets to work to fix with amazing energy:—

> "The Babe,
> Nursed in his Mother's arms, who sinks to sleep
> Rocked on his Mother's breast; who with his soul
> Drinks in the feelings of his Mother's eye!
> For him, in one dear Presence, there exists
> A virtue which irradiates and exalts
> Objects through widest intercourse of sense.
> No outcast he, bewildered and depressed:
> Along his infant veins are interfused
> The gravitation and the filial bond
> Of nature that connects him with the world."

He attaches his being to mother, father, sister, brother, 'nanna,' the man in the street whom he calls 'dada,' cat and dog, spider and fly; earth, air, fire, and water attract him perilously; his eyes covet light and colour, his ears sound, his limbs movement; everything concerns him, and out of everything he gets—

> "That calm delight
> Which, if I err not, surely must belong
> To those first-born affinities that fit
> Our new existence to existing things,
> And, in our dawn of being, constitute
> The bond of union between life and joy."

He gets also, when left to himself, the real knowledge about each thing which establishes his relation with that particular thing.

Our Part, to Remove Obstructions and to Give Stimulus

Later, we step in to educate him. In proportion to the range of living relationships we put in his way, will he have wide and vital interests, fullness of joy in living. In proportion as he is made aware of the laws which rule every relationship, will his life be dutiful and serviceable: as he learns that no relation with persons or with things, animate or inanimate, can be maintained without strenuous effort, will he learn the laws of work and the joys of work.

Our part is to remove obstructions and to give stimulus and guidance to the child who is trying to get into touch with the universe of things and thoughts which belongs to him.

Our Error

Our deadly error is to suppose that we are his showman to the universe; and, not only so, but that there is no community at all between child and universe unless such as we choose to set up. We are the people! and if we choose that a village child's education should be confined to the 'three R's,' why, what right has he to ask for more? If *life* means for him his Saturday night in the ale-house, surely that is not our fault! If our own boys go through school and college and come out without quickening interests, without links to the things that are worthwhile, we are not sure that it is our fault either. We resent that they should be called 'muddied oafs' because we know them to be fine fellows. So they are, splendid stuff which has not yet arrived at the making!

6

SELF EDUCATION

Diet for the body is abundantly considered, but no one pauses to say, "I wonder does the mind need food, too, and regular meals, and what is its proper diet?" I have asked myself this question and have laboured for fifty years to find the answer, and am anxious to impart what I think I know, but the answer cannot be given in the form of 'Do' this and that, but rather as an invitation to 'Consider' this and that; action follows when we have thought duly.

The life of the mind is sustained upon ideas; there is no intellectual vitality in the mind to which ideas are not presented several times, say, every day. But 'surely, surely,' as 'Mrs. Proudie' would say, scientific experiments, natural beauty, nature study, rhythmic movements, sensory exercises, are all fertile in ideas? Quite commonly, they are so, as regards ideas of invention and discovery; and even in ideas of art; but for the moment it may be well to consider the ideas that influence life, that is, character and conduct; these, would seem, pass directly from mind to mind, and are neither helped nor hindered by educational outworks.

Every child gets many of these ideas by word of mouth, by way of family traditions, proverbial philosophy,—in fact, by what we might call a kind of oral literature. But, when we compare the mind with the body, we perceive that three 'square' meals a day are generally necessary to health, and that a casual diet of ideas is poor and meagre. Our schools turn out a good many clever young persons, wanting in nothing but initiative, the power of reflection and the sort of moral imagination that enables you to 'put yourself in his place.' These qualities flourish upon a proper diet; and this is not afforded by the ordinary school book, or, in sufficient quantity by the ordinary lesson. I should like to emphasize quantity, which is as important for the mind as the body; both require their 'square meals.'

It is no easy matter to give its proper sustenance to the mind; hard things are said of children, that they have 'no brains,' 'a low order of intellect,' and so on; many of us are able to vouch for the fine intelligence shown by children who are fed with the proper mind-stuff; but teachers do not usually take the trouble to find out what this is. We come dangerously near to what Plato condemns as "that lie of the soul," that corruption of the highest truth, of which Protagoras is guilty in the saying that, "Knowledge is sensation." What else are we saying when we run after educational methods which are purely sensory? Knowledge is not sensation, nor is it to be derived through sensation; we feed upon the thoughts of other minds; and thought applied to thought generates thought and we become more thoughtful. No one need invite us to reason, compare, imagine; the mind, like the body, digests its proper food, and it must have the labour of digestion or it ceases to function.

But the children ask for bread and we give them a stone; we give information about objects and events which mind does not attempt to digest but casts out bodily (upon an examination paper?). But let information hang upon a principle, be inspired by an idea, and it is taken with avidity and used in making whatsoever in the spiritual nature stands for tissue in the physical.

"Education," said Lord Haldane, some time ago, "is a matter of the spirit,"—no wiser word has been said on the subject, and yet we persist in applying education from without as a bodily activity or emollient. We begin to see light. No one knoweth the things of a man but the spirit of a man which is in him; therefore, there is no education but self-education, and as soon as a young child begins his education he does so as a student. Our business is to give him mind-stuff, and both quality and quantity are essential. Naturally, each of us possesses this mind-stuff only in limited measure, but we know where to procure it; for the best thought the world possesses is stored in books; we must open books to children, the best books; our own concern is abundant provision and orderly serving.

I am jealous for the children; every modern educational movement tends to belittle them intellectually; and none more so than a late ingenious attempt to feed normal children with the pap-meat which may (?) be good for the mentally sick: but, "To all wildly popular things comes suddenly and inexorably death, without hope of resurrection." If Mr. Bernard Shaw is right, I need not discuss a certain popular form of 'New Education.' It has been ably said that education should profit by the divorce which is now in progress from psychology on the one hand and sociology on the other; but what if education should use her recovered liberty make a monstrous alliance with pathology?

Various considerations urge upon me a rather distasteful task. It is time I showed my hand and gave some account of work, the principles and practices of which should, I think, be of general use. Like those lepers who feasted at the gates of a famished city, I begin to take shame to myself! I have attempted to unfold (in various volumes) a system of educational theory which seems to me able to meet any rational demand, even that severest criterion set up by Plato; it is able to "run the gauntlet of objections, and is ready to disprove them, not by appeals to opinion, but to absolute truth." Some of it is new, much of it is old. Like the quality of mercy, it is not strained; certainly it is twice blessed, it blesses him that gives and him that takes, and a sort of radiancy of look distinguishes both scholar and teacher engaged in this manner of education; but there are no startling results to challenge attention.

Professor Bompas Smith remarked in an inaugural address at the University of Manchester that,—"If we can guide our practice by the light of a comprehensive theory we shall widen our experience by attempting tasks which would not otherwise have occurred to us." It is possible to offer the light of such a comprehensive theory, and the result is precisely what the Professor indicates,—a large number of teachers attempt tasks which would not otherwise have occurred to them. One discovers a thing because it is there, and no sane person takes credit to himself for such discovery. On the contrary, he recognizes with King Arthur,—"These jewels, whereupon I chanced Divinely, are for public use." For many years we have had access to a sort of Aladdin's cave which I long to throw open 'for public use.'

Let me try to indicate some of the advantages of the theory I am urging—It fits all ages, even the seven ages of man! It satisfies brilliant children and discovers intelligence in the dull. It secures attention, interest, concentration, without effort on the part of teacher or taught.

Children, I think, all children, so taught express themselves in forcible and fluent English and use a copious vocabulary. An unusual degree of nervous stability is attained; also, intellectual occupation seems to make for chastity in thought and life. Parents become interested in the schoolroom work, and find their children 'delightful companions.' Children shew delight in books (other than story books) and manifest a genuine love of knowledge. Teachers are relieved from much of the labour of corrections. Children taught according to this method do exceptionally well at any school. It is unnecessary to stimulate these young scholars by marks, prizes, etc.

Over thirty years ago I published a volume about the home education of children and people wrote asking how those counsels of perfection could be carried out with the aid of the private governess as she then existed; it occurred to me that a series of curricula might be devised embodying sound principles and securing that children should be in a position of less dependence on their teacher than they then were; in other words, that their education should be largely self-education. A sort of correspondence school was set up, the motto of which,—"I am, I can, I ought, I will," has had much effect in throwing children upon the possibilities, capabilities, duties and determining power belonging to them as persons.

"Children are born persons," is the first article of the educational credo in question. The response made by children (ranging in age from six to eighteen) astonished me; though they only shewed the power of attention, the avidity for knowledge, the clearness of thought, the nice discrimination in books, and the ability to deal with many subjects, for which I had given them credit in advance. I need not repeat what I have urged elsewhere on the subject of 'Knowledge' and will only add that anyone may apply a test; let him read to a child of any age from six to ten an account of an incident, graphically and tersely told, and the child will relate what he has heard point by point, though not word for word, and will add delightful original touches; what is more, he will relate the passage months later because he has visualised the scene and appropriated that bit of knowledge. A rhetorical passage, written in 'journalese,' makes no impression on him; if a passage be read more than once, he may become letter-perfect, but the spirit, the individuality has gone out of the exercise.

An older boy or girl will read one of Bacon's Essays, say, or a passage from De Quincey, and will write or tell it forcibly and with some style, either at the moment or months later. We know how Fox recited a whole pamphlet of Burke's at a College supper though he had probably read it no more than once. Here on the very surface is the key to that attention, interest, literary style, wide vocabulary, love of books, and readiness in speaking, which we all feel should belong to an education that is only begun at school and continued throughout life; these are the things that we all desire, and how to obtain them is some part of the open secret I am labouring to disclose 'for public use.'

I am anxious to bring a quite successful educational experiment before the public at a moment when we are told on authority that "Education must be . . . an appeal to the spirit if it is to be made interesting." Here is Education which is as interesting and fascinating as a fine art to parents, children and teachers.

During the last thirty years thousands of children educated on these lines have grown up in love with Knowledge and manifesting a 'right judgment in all things' so far as a pretty wide curriculum gives them data.

I would have children taught to read—to develop the habit of reading—before they learn the mechanical arts of reading and writing; and they learn delightfully; they give perfect attention to paragraph or page read to them and are able to relate the matter point by point, in their own words; but they demand classical English and cannot learn to read in this sense upon anything less. They begin their 'schooling' in 'letters' at six, and begin at the same time to learn mechanical reading and writing. A child does not lose by spending a couple of years in acquiring these because he is meanwhile 'reading' the Bible, history, geography, tales, with close attention and a remarkable power of reproduction, or rather, of translation into his own language; he is acquiring a copious vocabulary and the habit of consecutive speech. In a word, he is an educated child from the first, and his power of dealing with books, with several books in the course of a morning's 'school,' increases with his age.

But children are not all alike; there is as much difference between them as between men or women; two or three months ago, a small boy, not quite six, came to school (by post); and his record was that he could read anything in five languages, and was now teaching himself the Greek characters, could find his way about the Continental Bradshaw, and was a chubby, vigorous little person. All this the boy brings with him when he comes to school; he is exceptional, of course, just as a man with such accomplishments is exceptional; I believe that all children bring with them much capacity which is not recognized by their teachers, chiefly intellectual capacity, (always in advance of motor power), which we are apt to drown in deluges of explanation or dissipate in futile labours in which there is no advance.

People are naturally divided into those who read and think and those who do not read or think; and the business of schools is to see that all their scholars shall belong to the former class; it is worthwhile to remember that thinking is inseparable from reading which is concerned with the content of a passage and not merely with the printed matter.

The children I am speaking of are much occupied with things as well as with books, because 'Education is the Science of Relations,' is the principle which regulates their curriculum; that is, a child goes to school with many aptitudes which he should put into effect. So, he learns a good deal of science, because children have no difficulty in understanding principles, though technical details baffle them. He practises various handicrafts that he may know the feel of wood, clay, leather, and the joy of handling tools, that is, that he may establish a due relation with materials. But, always, it is the book, the knowledge, the clay, the bird or blossom, he thinks of, not his own place or his own progress.

I am afraid that some knowledge of the theory we advance is necessary to the open-minded teacher who would give our practices a trial, because every detail of schoolroom work is the outcome of certain principles. For instance, it would be quite easy, without much thought to experiment with our use of books; but in education, as in religion, it is the motive that counts, and the boy who reads his lesson for a 'good mark' becomes word-perfect, but does not know. But these principles are obvious and simple enough, and, when we consider that at present education is chaotic for want of a unifying theory, and that there happens to be no other comprehensive theory in the field which is in line with modern thought and fits every occasion, might it not be well to try one which is immediately practicable and always pleasant and has proved itself by producing many capable, serviceable, dutiful men and women of sound judgment and willing mind?

In urging a method of self-education for children in lieu of the vicarious education which prevails, I should like to dwell on the enormous relief to teachers, a self-sacrificing and greatly overburdened class; the difference is just that between driving a horse that is light and a horse that is heavy in hand; the former covers the ground of his own gay will and the driver goes merrily. The teacher who allows his scholars the freedom of the city of books is at liberty to be their guide, philosopher and friend; and is no longer the mere instrument of forcible intellectual feeding.

7

SCHOOL-BOOKS AND HOW THEY MAKE FOR EDUCATION

Line Upon Line

The theme of 'School-books' is not a new one, and I daresay the reader will find that I have said before what I shall say now. But we are not like those men of Athens who met to hear and to tell some new thing; and he will, I know, bear with me because he will recognise how necessary it is to repeat again and again counsels which are like waves beating against the rock of an accepted system of things. But, in time, the waves prevail and the rock wears away; so we go to work with good hope. Let me introduce what I have to say about school-books by a little story from an antiquated source.

An Incident of School-Girl Life

Frederika Bremer, in her novel of *The Neighbours*, tells an incident of school-girl life (possibly a bit of autobiography), with great spirit. Though it is rather long, I think the reader will thank me for it—the little episode advances what I have to say better than could any duller arguments of my own.

The heroine says:—

"I was then sixteen, and, fortunately for my restless character, my right shoulder began to project at the time. Gymnastics were then in fashion as remedies against all manner of defects, and my parents determined to let me try gymnastics. Arrayed in trimmed pantaloons, a Bonjour coat of green cloth and a little morning cap with pink ribbon, I made my appearance one day in an assemblage of from thirty to forty figures dressed almost the same as myself, who were merrily swarming about a large saloon, over ropes, ladders, and poles. It was a strange and novel scene.

"I kept myself in the background the first day, and learned from my governess the 'bending of the back' and the 'exercises of the arms and legs.' The second day I began to be intimate with some of the girls, the third I vied with them on ropes and ladders, and ere the close of the second week I was the leader of the second class, and began to encourage them to all manner of tricks.

"At that time I was studying Greek history; their heroes and their heroic deeds filled my imagination even in the gymnastic school. I proposed to my band to assume masculine and antique names and, in this place, to answer to no other than such as Agamemnon, Epaminondas, etc. For myself I chose the name of Orestes, and called my best friend in the class, Pylades. There was a tall thin girl, with a Finlandish accent, whom I greatly disliked, chiefly on account of the disrespect for me and my ideas which she manifested without reserve; . . . . from this arose fresh cause for quarrels.

"Although in love with the Greek history, I was no less taken with the Swedish. Charles XII was my idol, and I often entertained my friends in my class with narration of his deeds till my own soul was on fire with the most glowing enthusiasm. Like a shower of cold water, Darius (the tall girl, whose name was Britsa) one day came into the midst of us, and opposed me with the assertion that the Czar Peter I was a much greater man than Charles XII. I accepted the challenge with blind zeal and suppressed rage. My opponent brought forward a number of facts with coolness and skill, in support of her opinion, and when I, confuting all her positions, thought to exalt my victorious hero to the clouds, she was perpetually throwing Bender and Pultawa in my way. O Pultawa! Pultawa! many tears have fallen over thy bloody battlefield, but none more bitter than those which I shed in secret when I, like Charles himself, suffered a defeat there. Fuel was added to the flame until—'I challenge you, I demand satisfaction,' cried I to Darius, who only laughed and said, 'Bravo, bravo!' . . . I exclaimed, 'You have insulted me shamefully, and I request that you ask my pardon in the presence of the whole class, and acknowledge that Charles XII. was a greater man than Czar Peter, or else you shall fight with me, if you have any honour in your breast and are not a coward.'

"Britsa Kaijsa blushed, but said with detestable coolness: 'Ask pardon indeed? I should never dream of such a thing. Fight? O, yes, I have no objection! but where and with what? With pins, think you, or'—'With the sword if you are not afraid, and on this very spot. We can meet here half an hour before the rest; arms I shall bring with me; Pylades is my second and you shall appoint your own!' . . .

"Next morning when I had entered the spacious saloon, I found my enemy already there with her second. Darius and I saluted each other proudly and distantly. I gave her the first choice of the swords. She took one and flourished it about quite dexterously, as if she had been accustomed to the use of it. I saw myself (in imagination) already stabbed to the heart. 'Czar Peter *was* a great man,' cried Darius. 'Down with him! long life to Charles XII!' I cried, bursting into a furious rage.

"I placed myself in an attitude of defence. Darius did the same. . . . Our swords clashed one against the other, and in the next moment I was disarmed and thrown on the ground. Darius stood over me and I believed my last hour had arrived. How astonished was I, however, when my enemy threw her sword away from her, took me by the hand and lifted me up, whilst she cheerfully cried: 'Well, now you have satisfaction; let us be good friends again; you are a brave little body!' At this moment a tremendous noise was heard at the door and in rushed the fencing master and three teachers. My senses now forsook me."

I hope the reader is not among the naughty children who read the fable and skip the moral; for, whatever is to follow, is, in fact, the moral of this pretty incident.

How Did the Girls Get Their Enthusiasm?

What was it, we wonder, in their school-books that these Swedish maidens found so exciting? There is no hint of other than *school* reading. In the first place we may conclude it was *books*. The oral lesson for young children, the lecture for older, had not been invented in the earlier years of the last century. We use books in our schoolrooms; but one does not hear of wild enthusiasm, ungovernable excitement, over the tabulated events of the history books, the tabulated facts of the science primers. Those Swedish girls must have used books of another sort; and it is to our interest to find out of what sort. As records would be hard to come by, we must look for information to the girls themselves; not that we can summon them to give a direct answer, but if we can get at what *they* were, we shall be able to make a good guess at what should fire their souls.

What Manner of Book Sustains the Life of Thought?

The story discloses no more than that they were intelligent girls, probably the children of intelligent parents. But that is enough for our purpose. The question resolves itself into—What manner of book will find its way with upheaving effect into the mind of an intelligent boy or girl? We need not ask what the girl or boy likes. *She* very often likes the twaddle of goody-goody story books, *he* likes condiments, highly-spiced tales of adventure. We are all capable of liking mental food of a poor quality and a titillating nature; and possibly such food is good for us when our minds are in need of an elbow-chair; but our spiritual life is sustained on other stuff, whether we be boys or girls, men or women. By spiritual I mean that which is not corporeal; and which, for convenience sake, we call by various names—the life of thought, the life of feeling, the life of the soul.

It is curious how every inquiry, superficial as it may seem to begin with, leads us to fundamental principles. This simple-seeming question—what manner of school-books should our boys and girls use?—leads us straight to one of the two great principles which bottom educational thought.

The School-books of the Publishers

I believe that spiritual life, using spiritual in the sense I have indicated, is sustained upon only one manner of diet—the diet of ideas—the living progeny of living minds. Now, if we send to any publisher for his catalogue of school books, we find that it is accepted as the nature of a school-book that it be drained dry of living thought. It may bear the name of a thinker, but then it is the abridgment of an abridgment, and all that is left for the unhappy scholar is the dry bones of his subject denuded of soft flesh and living colour, of the stir of life and power of moving. Nothing is left but what Oliver Wendell Holmes calls the 'mere brute fact.'

It cannot be too often said that information is not education. You may answer an examination question about the position of the Seychelles and the Comoro Islands without having been anywise nourished by the fact of these island groups existing in such and such latitudes and longitudes; but if you follow Bullen in *The Cruise of the Cachelot* the names excite that little mental stir which indicates the reception of real knowledge.

Reason for Oral Teaching

Intelligent teachers are well aware of the dry-as-dust character of school books, so they fall back upon the 'oral' lesson, one of whose qualities must be that it is not *bookish*. Living ideas can be derived only from living minds, and so it occasionally happens that a vital spark is flashed from teacher to pupil. But this occurs only when the subject is one to which the teacher has given *original* thought. In most cases the oral lesson, or the more advanced lecture, consists of information got up by the teacher from various books, and imparted in language, a little pedantic, or a little commonplace, or a little reading-made-easy in style. At the best, the teacher is not likely to have vital interest in, and, consequently, original thought upon, a wide range of subjects.

Limitations of Teachers

We wish to place before the child open doors to many avenues of instruction and delight, in each one of which he should find quickening thoughts. We cannot expect a school to be manned by a dozen master-minds, and even if it were, and the scholar were taught by each in turn, it would be much to his disadvantage. What he wants of his teacher is moral and mental discipline, sympathy and direction; and it is better, on the whole, that the training of the pupil should be undertaken by one wise teacher than that he should be passed from hand to hand for this subject and that.

Our Aim in Education is to Give a Full Life

We begin to see what we want. Children make large demands upon us. We owe it to them to initiate an immense number of interests. 'Thou hast set my feet in a large room,' should be the glad cry of every intelligent soul. Life should be all *living*, and not merely a tedious passing of time; not all doing or all feeling or all thinking—the strain would be too great—but, all living; that is to say, we should be in touch wherever we go, whatever we hear, whatever we see, with some manner of vital interest. We cannot *give* the children these interests; we prefer that they should never say they have learned botany or conchology, geology or astronomy.

The question is not,—how much does the youth *know*? when he has finished his education—but how much does he *care*? and about how many orders of things does he care? In fact, how large is the room in which he finds his feet set? and, therefore, how full is the life he has before him? I know you may bring a horse to the water, but you cannot make him drink. What I complain of is that we do *not* bring our horse to the water. We give him miserable little text-books, mere compendiums of facts, which he is to learn off and say and produce at an examination; or we give him various knowledge in the form of warm diluents, prepared by his teacher with perhaps some grains of living thought to the gallon. And all the time we have books, books teeming with ideas fresh from the minds of thinkers upon every subject to which we can wish to introduce children.

We Undervalue Children

The fact is, we undervalue children. The notion that an infant is a huge oyster, who by slow degrees, and more and more, develops into that splendid intellectual and moral being, a full-grown man or woman, has been impressed upon us so much of late years that we believe intellectual spoon-meat to be the only food for what we are pleased to call 'little minds.' It is nothing to us that William Morris read his first Waverley Novel when he was four and had read the whole series by the time he was seven. He did not die of it, but lived and prospered; unlike that little Richard, son of John Evelyn, who died when he was five years and three days old, a thing not to be wondered at when we read that he had 'a strong passion for Greek, could turn English into Latin and *vice versa* with the greatest ease,' had 'a wonderful disposition to Mathematics, having by heart divers propositions of Euclid'; but I quote little Richard (nobody could ever have called him Dick) by way of warning and not of example. Baron Macaulay [author of *History of England*] seems to have begun life as a great reader. We know the delightful story of how, when Hannah More called on his parents, he, a little boy of four, came forward with pretty hospitality to say that if she 'would be good enough to come in' he would bring her 'a glass of old spirits.' He explained afterwards that 'Robinson Crusoe often had some.'

Children of the Last Generation

But we may dismiss these precocious or exceptional children. All we ask of them is to remind us that our grandfathers and grandmothers recognised children as reasonable beings, persons of mind and conscience like themselves; but, needing their guidance and control, as having neither knowledge nor experience. Witness the queer old children's books which have come down to us; these addressed children as, before all things, reasonable, intelligent, and responsible persons. This is the note of home-life in the last generation. So soon as the baby realised his surroundings, he found himself morally and intellectually responsible.

Children as They Are

And children have not altered. This is how we find them—with intelligence more acute, logic more keen, observing powers more alert, moral sensibilities more quick, love and faith and hope more abounding; in fact, in all points like as we are, only more so; but absolutely ignorant of the world and its belongings, of us and our ways, and, above all, of how to control and direct and manifest the infinite possibilities with which they are born.

Our Work, to Give Vitalising Ideas

Knowing that the brain is the physical seat of habit and that conduct and character, alike, are the outcome of the habits we allow; knowing, too, that an inspiring idea initiates a new habit of thought, and hence, a new habit of life; we perceive that the great work of education is to inspire children with vitalising ideas as to every relation of life, every department of knowledge, every subject of thought; and to give deliberate care to the formation of those habits of the good life which are the outcome of vitalising ideas. In this great work we seek and assuredly find the co-operation of the Divine Spirit, whom we recognise, in a sense rather new to modern thought, as the supreme Educator of mankind in things that have been called secular, fully as much as in those that have been called sacred.

8

HOW TO USE SCHOOL-BOOKS

Disciplinary Subjects of Instruction

Having cleared our minds as to the end we have in view, we ask ourselves—'Is there any fruitful idea underlying this or that study that the children are engaged in?' We divest ourselves of the notion that to develop the faculties is the chief thing, and a 'subject' which does not rise out of some great thought of life we usually reject as not nourishing, not fruitful; while we retain those studies which give exercise in habits of clear and orderly thinking. Mathematics, grammar, logic, etc., are not purely disciplinary, they do develop intellectual muscle. We by no means reject the familiar staples of education in the school sense, but we prize them even more for the record of intellectual habits they leave in the brain tissue, than for their distinct value in developing certain 'faculties.'

'Open, Sesame'

I think we should have a great educational revolution once we ceased to regard ourselves as assortments of so-called faculties, and realised ourselves as persons whose great business it is to get in touch with other persons of all sorts and condition; of all countries and climes, of all times, past and present. History would become entrancing, literature a magic mirror for the discovery of other minds, the study of sociology a duty and a delight. We should tend to become responsive and wise, humble and reverent, recognising the duties and the joys of the full human life. We cannot of course overtake such a programme of work, but we can keep it in view; and I suppose every life is moulded upon its ideal.

The Bible, the Great Storehouse of Moral Impression

Valuable as are some compendiums of its moral teaching, it is to the Bible itself we must go as to the great storehouse of moral impressions. Let us hear De Quincey on this subject:—

"It had happened, that among our vast nursery collection of books was the Bible, illustrated with many pictures. And in long dark evenings, as my three sisters with myself sat by the firelight round the guard of our nursery, no book was so much in request amongst us. It ruled us and swayed us as mysteriously as music. Our younger nurse, whom we all loved, would sometimes, according to her simple powers, endeavour to explain what we found obscure. We, the children, were all constitutionally touched with pensiveness; the fitful gloom and sudden lambencies of the room by firelight suited our evening state of feelings; and they suited also, the divine revelations of power and mysterious beauty which awed us.

"Above all, the story of a just man—man and yet not man, real above all things, and yet shadowy above all things—who had suffered the passion of death in Palestine, slept upon our minds like early dawn upon the waters. The nurse knew and explained to us the chief differences in oriental climates; and all these differences (as it happens) express themselves, more or less, in varying relation to the great accidents and powers of summer. The cloudless sunlights of Syria—these seemed to argue everlasting summer; the disciples plucking the ears of corn—that *must* be summer; but, above all, the very name of Palm Sunday (a festival in the English Church) troubled me like an anthem."

Effect of Our Liturgy on a Child

I cannot refrain from adding De Quincey's beautiful words describing the effect of our liturgy upon him as a child. "On Sunday mornings I went with the rest of my family to church: it was a church on the ancient model of England, having aisles, galleries, organ, all things ancient and venerable, and the proportions majestic. Here, whilst the congregation knelt through the long litany, as often as we came to that passage, so beautiful amongst many that are so, where God is supplicated on behalf of 'all sick persons and young children,' and that He would 'show His pity upon all prisoners and captives,' I wept in secret; and raising my streaming eyes to the upper windows of the galleries, saw, on days when the sun was shining, a spectacle as affecting as ever prophet can have beheld. The *sides* of the windows were rich with stained glass; through the deep purples and crimsons streamed the golden light; emblazonries of heavenly illumination (from the sun) mingling with the earthly emblazonries (from art and its gorgeous colouring) of what is grandest in man. *There* were the apostles that had trampled upon earth, and the glories of earth, out of celestial love to man. *There* were the martyrs that had borne witness to the truth through flames, through torments, and through armies of fierce, insulting faces. *There* were the saints who, under intolerable pangs, had glorified God by meek submission to His will." "God speaks to children, also, in dreams and by the oracles that lurk in darkness. But in *solitude*, above all things, when made vocal to the meditative heart by the truths and services of a national church, God holds with children 'communion undisturbed.' *Solitude*, though it may be silent as light, is, like light, the mightiest of agencies; for solitude is essential to man. All men come into this world *alone*; all leave it *alone*."

Principles on Which to Select School-books

In their power of giving impulse and stirring emotion is another use of books, the right books; but that is just the question—which *are* the right books?—a point upon which I should not wish to play Sir Oracle. The 'hundred best books for the schoolroom' may be put down on a list, but not by me. I venture to propose one or two principles in the matter of school-books, and shall leave the far more difficult part, the application of those principles, to the reader. For example, I think we owe it to children to let them dig their knowledge, of whatever subject, for themselves out of the fit book; and this for two reasons: What a child *digs for* is his own possession; what is poured into his ear, like the idle song of a pleasant singer, floats out as lightly as it came in, and is rarely assimilated. I do not mean to say that the lecture and the oral lesson are without their uses; but these uses are, to give impulse and to *order* knowledge; and not to convey knowledge, or to afford us that part of our education which comes of fit knowledge, fitly given.

Again, as I have already said, ideas must reach us directly from the mind of the thinker, and it is chiefly by means of the books they have written that we get into touch with the best minds.

Marks of a Fit Book

As to the distinguishing marks of a book for the school-room, a word or two may be said. A fit book is not necessarily a big book. John Quincy Adams, aged nine, wrote to his father for the fourth volume of Smollett for his private reading, though, as he owned up, his thoughts were running on birds' eggs; and perhaps some of us remember going religiously through the many volumes of Alison's *History of Europe* with a private feeling that the bigness of the book swelled the virtue of the reader. But, now, big men write little books, to be used with discretion; because sometimes the little books are no more than abstracts, the dry bones of the subjects; and sometimes the little books are fresh and living. Again, we need not always insist that a book should be written by the original thinker. It sometimes happens that second-rate minds have assimilated the matter in hand, and are able to give out what is their own thought (only because they have *made* it their own) in a form more suitable for our purpose than that of the first-hand thinkers. We cannot make any hard and fast rule—a big book or a little book, a book at first-hand or at second-hand; either may be right provided we have it in us to discern a *living* book, quick, and informed with the ideas proper to the subject of which it treats.

How to Use the Right Books

So much for the right books; the right use of them is another matter. The children must enjoy the book. The ideas it holds must each make that sudden, delightful impact upon their minds, must cause that intellectual stir, which mark the inception of an idea. The teacher's part in this regard is to see and feel for himself, and then to rouse his pupils by an appreciative look or word; but to beware how he deadens the impression by a flood of talk. Intellectual sympathy is very stimulating; but we have all been in the case of the little girl who said, "Mother, I think I could understand if you did not explain *quite* so much." A teacher said of her pupil, "I find it so hard to tell whether she has really grasped a thing or whether she has only got the mechanical hang of it" Children are imitative monkeys, and it is the 'mechanical hang' that is apt to arrive after a douche of explanation.

Children Must Labour

This, of getting ideas out of them, is by no means all we must do with books. 'In all labour there is profit,' at any rate in some labour; and the labour of thought is what his book must induce in the child. He must generalise, classify, infer, judge, visualise, discriminate, labour in one way or another, with that capable mind of his, until the substance of his book is assimilated or rejected, according as he shall determine; for the determination rests with him and not with his teacher.

Value of Narration

The simplest way of dealing with a paragraph or a chapter is to require the child to narrate its contents after a single attentive reading,—one reading, however slow, should be made a condition; for we are all too apt to make sure we shall have another opportunity of finding out 'what 'tis all about' There is the weekly review if we fail to get a clear grasp of the news of the day; and, if we fail a second time, there is a monthly or a quarterly review or an annual summing up: in fact, many of us let present-day history pass by us with easy minds, feeling sure that, in the end, we shall be *compelled* to see the bearings of events. This is a bad habit to get into; and we should do well to save our children by not giving them the vague expectation of second and third and tenth opportunities to do that which should have been done at first.

A Single Careful Reading

There is much difference between intelligent reading, which the pupil should do in silence, and a mere parrot-like cramming up of contents; and it is not a bad test of education to be able to give the points of a description, the sequence of a series of incidents, the links in a chain of argument, correctly, after a single careful reading. This is a power which a barrister, a publisher, a scholar, labours to acquire; and it is a power which children can acquire with great ease, and once acquired, the gulf is bridged which divides the reading from the non-reading community.

Other Ways of Using Books

But this is only one way to use books: others are to enumerate the statements in a given paragraph or chapter; to analyse a chapter, to divide it into paragraphs under proper headings, to tabulate and classify series; to trace cause to consequence and consequence to cause; to discern character and perceive how character and circumstance interact; to get lessons of life and conduct, or the living knowledge which makes for science, out of books; all this is possible for school boys and girls, and *until* they have begun to use books for themselves in such ways, they can hardly be said to have begun their education.

The Teacher's Part

The teacher's part is, in the first place, to see what is to be done, to look over the work of the day in advance and see what mental discipline, as well as what vital knowledge, this and that lesson afford; and then to set such questions and such tasks as shall give full scope to his pupils' mental activity. Let marginal notes be freely made, as neatly and beautifully as may be, for books should be handled with reverence. Let numbers, letters, underlining be used to help the eye and to save the needless fag of writing abstracts. Let the pupil write for himself half a dozen questions which cover the passage studied; he need not write the answers if he be taught that the mind can know nothing but what it can produce in the form of an answer to a question put by the mind to itself.

Disciplinary Devices Must Not Come Between Children and the Soul of the Book

These few hints by no means cover the disciplinary uses of a good school-book; but let us be careful that our disciplinary devices, and our mechanical devices to secure and tabulate the substance of knowledge, do not come between the children and that which is the *soul* of the book, the living thought it contains. Science is doing so much for us in these days, nature is drawing so close to us, art is unfolding so much meaning to us, the world is becoming so rich for us, that we are a little in danger of neglecting the art of deriving sustenance from books.

Let us not in such wise impoverish our lives and the lives of our children; for, to quote the golden words of Milton: "Books are not absolutely dead things, but do contain a potency of life in them to be as active as that soul was, whose progeny they are; nay, they do preserve, as in a vial, the purest efficacy and extraction of that living intellect that bred them. As good almost kill a man, as kill a good book; who kills a man kills a good reasonable creature, God's image; but he who destroys a good book, kills reason itself—kills the image of God, as it were, in the eye."

9

READING FOR OLDER CHILDREN

In teaching to read, as in other matters, *c'est le premier pas qui coute*. The child who has been taught to read with care and deliberation until he has mastered the words of a limited vocabulary, usually does the rest for himself. The attention of his teachers should be fixed on two points—that he acquires the habit of reading, and that he does not fall into slipshod habits of reading.

The Habit of Reading

The most common and the monstrous defect in the education of the day is that children fail to acquire the habit of reading. Knowledge is conveyed to them by lessons and talk, but the studious habit of using books as a means of interest and delight is not acquired. This habit should be begun early; so soon as the child can read at all, he should read for himself, and to himself, history, legends, fairy tales, and other suitable matter. He should be trained from the first to think that one reading of any lesson is enough to enable him to narrate what he has read, and will thus get the habit of slow, careful reading, intelligent even when it is silent, because he reads with an eye to the full meaning of every clause.

Reading Aloud

He should have practice, too, in reading aloud, for the most part, in the books he is using for his term's work. These should include a good deal of poetry, to accustom him to the delicate rendering of shades of meaning, and especially to make him aware that words are beautiful in themselves, that they are a source of pleasure, and are worthy of our honour; and that a beautiful word deserves to be beautifully said, with a certain roundness of tone and precision of utterance. Quite young children are open to this sort of teaching, conveyed, not in a lesson, but by a word now and then.

Limitation

In this connection the teacher should not trust to setting, as it were, a copy in reading for the children's imitation. They do imitate readily enough, catching tricks of emphasis and action in an amusing way; but these are mere tricks, an aping of intelligence. The child must express what he feels to be the author's meaning; and this sort of intelligent reading comes only of the habit of reading with understanding.

Reading to Children

It is a delight to older people to read aloud to children, but this should be only an occasional treat and indulgence, allowed before bedtime, for example. We must remember the natural inertness of a child's mind; give him the habit of being read to, and he will steadily shirk the labour of reading for himself; indeed, we all like to be spoon-fed with our intellectual meat, or we should read and think more for ourselves and be less eager to run after lectures.

Questions on the Subject-Matter

When a child is reading, he should not be teased with questions as to the meaning of what he has read, the signification of this word or that; what is annoying to older people is equally annoying to children. Besides, it is not of the least consequence that they should be able to give the meaning of every word they read. A knowledge of meanings, that is, an ample and correct vocabulary, is only arrived at in one way—by the habit of reading. A child unconsciously gets the meaning of a new word from the context, if not the first time he meets with it, then the second or the third: but he is on the look-out, and will find out for himself the sense of any expression he does not understand.

Direct questions on the subject-matter of what a child has read are always a mistake. Let him narrate what he has read, or some part of it. He enjoys this sort of consecutive reproduction, but abominates every question in the nature of a riddle. If there must be riddles, let it be his to ask and the teacher's to direct him the answer. Questions that lead to a side issue or to a personal view are allowable because these interest children—'What would you have done in his place?'

Lesson-Books

A child has not begun his education until he has acquired the habit of reading to himself, with interest and pleasure, books fully on a level with his intelligence. I am speaking now of his lesson-books, which are all too apt to be written in a style of insufferable twaddle, probably because they are written by persons who have never chanced to meet a child. All who know children know that they do not talk twaddle and do not like it, and prefer that which appeals to their understanding.

Their lesson-books should offer matter for their reading, whether aloud or to themselves; therefore they should be written with literary power. As for the matter of these books, let us remember that children can take in ideas and principles, whether the latter be moral or mechanical, as quickly and clearly as we do ourselves (perhaps more so); but detailed processes, lists and summaries, blunt the edge of a child's delicate mind.

Therefore, the selection of their first lesson-books is a matter of grave importance, because it rests with these to give children the idea that knowledge is supremely attractive and that reading is delightful. Once the habit of reading his lesson-book with delight is set up in a child, his education is—not completed, but—ensured; he will go on for himself in spite of the obstructions which school too commonly throws in his way.

Slipshod Habits; Inattention

I have already spoken of the importance of a single reading. If a child is not able to narrate what he has read once, let him not get the notion that he may, or that he must, read it again. A look of slight regret because there is a gap in his knowledge will convict him. The power of reading with perfect attention will not be gained by the child who is allowed to moon over his lessons. For this reason, reading lessons must be short; ten minutes or a quarter of an hour of fixed attention is enough for children of the ages we have in view, and a lesson of this length will enable a child to cover two or three pages of his book. The same rule as to the length of a lesson applies to children whose lessons are read to them because they are not yet able to read for themselves.

10

THE LOVE OF KNOWLEDGE

The Use of Books Makes for Short Hours

Considering that under the head of 'Education by Books' some half-dozen groups of subjects are included, with several subjects in each group, the practical teacher will be inclined to laugh at what will seem to him Education in Utopia. In practice, however, we find that the use of books makes for short hours. No book-work or writing, no preparation or report, is done in the *Parents'* *Review* School, except between the hours of 9 and 11.30 for the lowest class, to 9 and 1 for the highest, with half an hour's interval for Swedish Drill [a form of physical exercise], etc.

From one to two hours, according to age and class, are given in the afternoons to handicrafts, field-work, drawing, etc.; and the evenings are absolutely free, so that the children have leisure for hobbies, family reading, and the like. We are able to get through a greater variety of subjects, and through more work in each subject, in a shorter time than is usually allowed, because children taught in this way get the habit of close attention and are carried on by steady interest.

'Utilitarian' Education

I should be inclined to say of education, as Mr. Lecky says of morals, that "the Utilitarian theory is profoundly immoral." To educate children for any immediate end—towards commercial or manufacturing aptitude, for example—is to put a premium upon general ignorance with a view to such special aptitude. The greater includes the less, but the less does not include the greater. Excellent work of whatever kind is produced by a person of character and intelligence, and we who teach cannot do better for the nation than to prepare such persons for its uses. He who has intelligent relations with life will produce good work.

Relations and Interests

I have throughout spoken of *'Relations,'* and not of *'Interests,'* because interests may be casual, unworthy, and passing. Everyone, even the most ignorant, has interests of a sort; while to make valid any one relation, implies that knowledge has begun in, at any rate, that one direction. But the defect in our educational thought is that we have ceased to realise that knowledge is vital; and, as children and adults, we suffer from underfed minds. This intellectual inanition is, no doubt, partly due to the fact that educational theorists systematically depreciate knowledge. Such theorists are, I think, inclined to attach more importance to the working of the intellectual machinery than to the output of the product; that is, they feel it to be more important that a child should *think* than that he should *know*. My contention is rather that he cannot *know* without having *thought;* and also that he cannot think without an abundant, varied, and regular supply of the material of knowledge. We all know how the reading of a passage may stimulate in us thought, inquiry, inference, and thus get for us in the end some added knowledge.

The depreciation of which I speak is by no means of set purpose, nor is it even realised; but the more education presents itself as a series of psychological problems, the greater will be the tendency to doctor, modify, and practically eliminate *knowledge;*— that knowledge, which is as the air, and the food, and the exercise, the whole life of the mind of man. In giving 'education' without abundant knowledge, we are as persons who should aim at physical development by giving the maximum of exercise with the minimum of food. The getting of knowledge and the getting of delight in knowledge are the ends of a child's education; and well has said one of our prophets [*Carlyle*], "that there should one man die ignorant who had capacity for knowledge, this I call a tragedy." To sum up, I believe that our efforts at intellectual education commonly fail from six causes:

Causes of Failure

(a) The oral lesson, which at its worst is very poor twaddle, and at its best is far below the ordered treatment of the same subject by an original mind in the right book. (The right books exist, old and new, in countless numbers, but very great care is necessary in the choice, as well as much experience of the rather whimsical tastes and distastes of children.)

(b) The lecture, commonly gathered from various books in rapid notes by the teacher; and issuing in hasty notes, afterwards written out, and finally crammed up by the pupils. The lecture is often careful, thorough, and well-illustrated; but is it ever equal in educational value to direct contact with the original mind of one able thinker who has written his book on the subject? Arnold, Thring, Bowen, we know, lectured with great effect, but then each of them lectured on only a few subjects, and each lecture was as the breaking out of a spring of slowly gathered knowledge. We are not all Arnolds or even Bowens.

(c) The text-book, compressed and re-compressed from one or many big books. These handbooks are of two kinds—the frankly dry and uninteresting, which enumerate facts and details; and the easy and beguiling. I think we are safe in saying that there is *no educational value* in either sort of text-book.

(d) The debauchery of the mind which comes of exciting other desires to do the work of the inherent and fully adequate desire of knowledge.

(e) In elementary schools, the dependence upon apparatus and illustrative appliances which have a paralysing effect on the mind.

(f) Again in elementary schools, the use of 'Readers,' which, however well selected, cannot have the value of consecutive works.

Education by Books

For the last twelve years we have tried the plan of bringing children up on *Books* and *Things*, and, on the whole, the results are pleasing. The *average* child studies with 'delight.' We do not say he will remember all he knows, but, to use a phrase of Jane Austen's, he will have had his 'imagination warmed' in many regions of knowledge.

Let us, out of reverence for the children, be modest; let us not stake their interests on the hope that this or that new way would lead to great results if people had only the courage to follow it. It is exciting to become a pioneer; but, for the children's sake, it may be well to constrain ourselves to follow those roads only by which we know that persons have arrived, or those newer roads which offer evident and assured means of *progress towards a desired end.* Self-will is not permitted to the educationalist; and he may not take up fads.

An Educated Child

Knowledge is, no doubt, a comparative term, and the knowledge of a subject possessed by a child would be the ignorance of a student. All the same, there is such a thing as an educated child—a child who possesses a sound and wide knowledge of a number of subjects, all of which serve to interest him; such a child studies with 'delight.'

Children Delight in School, but Not for Love of Knowledge

It will be said with truth that most children delight in school; they delight in the stimulus of school life, in the social stir of companionship; they are emulous, eager for reward and praise; they enjoy the thousand lawful interests of school life, including the attractive personality of such and such a teacher; but it seems doubtful whether the love of knowledge, in itself and for itself; is usually a powerful motive with the young scholar. The matter is important, because, of all the joyous motives of school life, the love of knowledge is the only abiding one; the only one which determines the scale, so to speak, upon which the person will hereafter live. My contention is, to repeat what has been said, that all children have a capacity for and a latent love of knowledge; and, that knowledge concerning persons and States can best be derived from books, and should be got by the children out of their own books.

In a hundred biographies there are hints of boys and girls who have grown up on books; and there is no doubt that in many schools the study of books is the staple of the work. This probably is the principle which keeps our great public schools perennially alive; they live, so far as they do live, upon books. The best public schoolboy is a fine product; and perhaps the worst has had his imagination touched by ideas; yet most of us recognise that the public school often fails, in that it launches the average and dull boy ignorant upon the world because the curriculum has been too narrow to make any appeal to him.

And we must remember, that if a young person leave school at seventeen or eighteen without having become a diligent and delighted reader, it is tolerably certain that he will never become a reader, it may be, however, that the essential step in any reform of public schools should come in the shape of due *preparation* upon a wide curriculum, dealt with intelligently, between the ages of six and twelve.

An Educational Revolution

I add appendices to show, (a) how a wide curriculum and the use of many books work in the *Parents' Review* School; (b) what progress a pupil of twelve should have made under such conditions; and (c) what use is made of oral lessons. Should the reader consider that the children in question prove their right of entry to several fields of knowledge, that they show a distinct appetite for such knowledge, that thought and power of mind develop upon the books we read, as they do not and cannot upon the lectures we hear; should he indeed be convinced of the truth of what I have advanced, I think he will see that, not an educational reform here and there, but an *Educational Revolution* is before us to which every one of us is bound to put his hand.

The Children's Magna Carta

My plea is, and I think I have justified it by experience, that many doors shall be opened to boys and girls until they are at least twelve or fourteen, and always the doors of good houses, ('Education,' says Taine, 'is but a card of invitation to noble and privileged salons'); that they shall be introduced to no subject whatever through compendiums, abstracts, or selections; that the young people shall learn what history is, what literature is, what life is, from the living books of those who know. I know it can be done, because it is being done on a considerable scale.

If conviction has indeed reached us, the Magna Carta of children's intellectual liberty is before us. The need is immediate, the means are evident. This, least, I think we ought to claim, that, up to the age of twelve, all boys and girls shall be educated on some such curriculum, with some such *habit* of *Books* as we have been considering.

11

A SAMPLE CURRICULUM: LITERATURE

The Knowledge of Man

Except in Form I the study of Literature goes pari passu with that of History. Fairy tales, (Andersen or Grimm, for example), delight Form lB, and the little people re-tell these tales copiously, vividly, and with the astonishing exactness we may expect when we remember how seriously annoyed they are with the story-teller who alters a phrase or a circumstance. *Aesop's Fables*, too, are used with great success, and are rendered, after being once heard, with brevity and point, and children readily appropriate the moral. Mrs. Gatty's *Parables From Nature*, again, serve another purpose. They feed a child's sense of wonder and are very good to tell. There is no attempt to reduce the work of this form, or any other, to a supposed 'child level.' Form IA (7 to 9) hears and tells chapter by chapter *The Pilgrim's Progress* and the children's narrations are delightful. No beautiful thought or bold figure escapes them. Andrew Lang's *Tales of Troy and Greece*, a big volume, is a *piece de resistance* going on from term to term.

The great tales of the heroic age find their way to children's hearts. They conceive vividly and tell eagerly, and the difficult classical names. instead of being a stumbling-block, are a delight, because, as a Master of a Council school says,—

> "Children have an instinctive power by which they are able to sense the meaning of a whole passage and even some difficult words."

That the sonorous beauty of these classical names appeals to them is illustrated by a further quotation from the same Master,—

> "A boy of about seven in my school the other day asked his mother why she had not given him one of those pretty names they heard in the stories at school. He thought Ulysses a prettier name than his own, Kenneth, and that the mother of his playmate might have called him Achilles instead of Alan."

There is profound need to cultivate delight in beautiful names in days when we are threatened with the fear that London itself should lose that rich halo of historic associations which glorifies its every street and alley, that it may be made like New York, and should name a street X500,—like a workhouse child without designation; an age when we express the glory and beauty of the next highest peak of the Himalayas by naming it D2! In such an age, this, of their inherent aptitude for beautiful names, is a lode of much promise in children's minds. The Kaffir who announced that his name was' Telephone' had an ear for sound. Kingsley's *Water Babies*, Carroll's *Alice in Wonderland*, Kipling's *Just So Stories*, scores of exquisite classics written for children, but not written down to them, are suitable at this stage.

Form IIB has a considerable programme of reading, that is, not the mere mechanical exercise of reading but the reading of certain books. Therefore it is necessary that two years should be spent in Form IA and that in the second of these two years the children should read a good deal of the set work for themselves. In IIB they read their own geography, history, poetry, but perhaps Shakespeare's *Twelfth Night*, say, Scott's *Rob Roy*, Swift's *Gulliver's Travels*, should be read to them and narrated by them until they are well in their tenth year. Their power to understand, visualise, and 'tell' a play of Shakespeare from nine years old and onwards is very surprising. They put in nothing which is not there, but they miss nothing and display a passage or a scene in a sort of curious relief. One or two books of the calibre of *The Heroes of Asgard* are also included in the programme for the term.

The transition to Form IIA is marked by more individual reading as well as by a few additional books. The children read their 'Shakespeare play' in character. Certain Council School boys, we are told, insist on dramatising Scott as they read it. Bulfinch's *Age of Fable* admits them to the rich imaginings of peoples who did not yet know. Goldsmith's poems and Stevenson's *Kidnapped*, etc., may form part of a term's work, and in each and all children shew the same surprising power of knowing, evinced by the one sure test,—they are able to 'tell' each work they have read not only with accuracy but with spirit and originality. How is it possible, it may be asked, to show originality in 'mere narration'? Let us ask Scott, Shakespeare, Homer, who told what they knew, that is narrated, but with continual scintillations from their own genius playing upon the written word. Just so in their small degree do the children narrate; they see it all so vividly that when you read or hear their versions the theme is illuminated for you, too.

Children remain in Form II until they are twelve, and here I would remark on the evenness with which the power of children in dealing with books is developed. We spread an abundant and delicate feast in the programmes and each small guest assimilates what he can. The child of genius and imagination gets greatly more than his duller comrade but all sit down to the same feast and each one gets according to his needs and powers.

The surprises afforded by the dull and even the 'backward' children are encouraging and illuminating. We think we know that man is an educable being, but when we afford to children all that they want we discover how straitened were our views, how poor and narrow the education we offered. Even in so-called deficient children we perceive,—

"What a piece of work is man . . . In apprehension, how like a god!"

In Forms III and IV we introduce a *History of English Literature* carefully chosen to afford sympathetic interest and delight while avoiding stereotyped opinions and stale information. The portion read each term (say fifty pages) corresponds with the period covered in history studies and the book is a great favourite with children. They have of course a great flair for Shakespeare, whether *King Lear*, *Twelfth Night*, *Henry V*, or some other play, and The Waverleys usually afford a contemporary tale.

There has been discussion in Elementary Schools as to whether an abridged edition would not give a better chance of getting through the novel set for a term, but strong arguments were brought forward at a conference of teachers in Gloucester in favour of a complete edition. Children take pleasure in the 'dry' parts, descriptions and the like, rendering these quite beautifully in their narrations.

Form IV may have quite a wide course of reading. For instance if the historical period for a term include the Commonwealth, they may read *L'Allegro*, and *Il Penseroso*, *Lycidas*, and contemporary poets as represented in a good anthology, or, for a later period, Pope's *Rape of the Lock*, or Gray's poems, while Form III read poems of Goldsmith and Burns. The object of children's literary studies is not to give them precise information as to who wrote what in the reign of whom?—but to give them a sense of the spaciousness of the days, not only of great Elizabeth, but of all those times of which poets, historians and the makers of tales, have left us living pictures.

In such ways the children secure, not the sort of information which is of little cultural value, but wide spaces wherein imagination may take those holiday excursions deprived of which life is dreary; judgment, too, will turn over these folios of the mind and arrive at fairly just decisions about a given strike, the question of Poland, Indian Unrest. Every man is called upon to be a statesman seeing that every man and woman, too, has a share in the government of the country; but statesmanship requires imaginative conceptions, formed upon pretty wide reading and some familiarity with historical precedents.

The reading for Forms V and VI (ages 15 to 18) is more comprehensive and more difficult. Like that in the earlier Forms, it follows the lines of the history they are reading, touching current literature in the occasional use of modern books; but young people who have been brought up on this sort of work may, we find, be trusted to keep themselves *au fait* with the best that is being produced in their own days. Given the proper period, Form V would cover in a term Pope's *Essay on Man*, Carlyle's *Essay on Burns*, Frankfort Moore's *Jessamy Bride*, Goldsmith's *Citizen of the World*, Thackeray's *The Virginians*, the contemporary poets from an anthology. Form VI would read Boswell, *The Battle of the Books*, Macaulay's *Essays* on Goldsmith, Johnson, Pitt; the contemporary poets from *The Oxford Book of Verse*, and both Forms read *She Stoops to Conquer*. This course of reading, it will be seen, is suggestive and will lead to much reading round and about it in later days.

As for the amount covered in each Form, it is probably about the amount most of us cover in the period of time included in a school term, but while we grown-up persons read and forget because we do not take the pains to know as we read, these young students have the powers of perfect recollection and just application because they have read with attention and concentration and have in every case reproduced what they have read in narration, or, the gist of some portion of it, in writing.

The children's answers in their examination papers, show that literature has become a living power in the minds of these young people.

ABOUT THE EDITOR

Deborah Taylor-Hough, long-time homeschooling mother of three (now adult) children, is the author of a number of books including *A Twaddle-Free Education: An Introduction to Charlotte Mason's Timeless Educational Ideas* (Simple Pleasures Press), *Frugal Living For Dummies*® (Wiley), and the bestselling *Frozen Assets* cookbook series (SourceBooks). Debi has also worked as Outreach Director and Youth Director at her church, and regularly teaches classes, workshops and seminars throughout the USA and Canada to women's groups, conferences, churches, and community education programs.

Debi's workshop topics include:

- Charlotte Mason home education
- living within your means
- simple living
- cooking for the freezer
- general homemaking
- writing, publishing, and publicity
- identifying personal priorities
- simplifying the holidays
- easy educational ideas for children
- … and lots more!

Visit Debi online:

CharlotteMasonHome.com
AFrugalSimpleLife.com

Also available from Deborah Taylor-Hough:

Frozen Assets: Cook for a Day, Eat for a Month
ISBN: 9781402218590 (Sourcebooks)

This breakthrough cookbook delivers a program for readers to cook a week or a month's worth of meals in just one day by using easy and affordable recipes to create a customized meal plan. The author, who saved $24,000 on her family's total grocery bill during a five-year period, offers up kid-tested and family approved recipes in Frozen Assets, plus bulk-cooking tips for singles, shopping lists, recipes for two-week and 30-day meal plans, and a ten-day plan to eliminate cooking over the holidays. Cooking for the freezer allows you to plan ahead, purchase items in bulk, cut down on waste, and stop those all-too-frequent trips to the drive-thru.

Frozen Assets Lite and Easy
ISBN: 9781402218606 (Sourcebooks)

Taylor-Hough is back with a book of low-fat, lower-calorie meal plans that use the same time-saving and cost-effective methods. *Frozen Assets Lite and Easy* shows readers how to eat healthy food while still saving time and money, with shopping lists, recipes, and detailed instruction on how to make freezer cooking work for you.

Frugal Living For Dummies®
ISBN: 9780764554032 (Wiley)

Need help keeping that New Year's resolution to eliminate credit card debt and live within your means? Packed with tips on cutting costs on everything from groceries to gifts for all occasions, this practical guide shows you how to spend less on the things you need and save more for those fun things you want.